i want to be an artist!

by david j landry
copyright 2018

for ages 2 - 200

So...
you want to be an artist?

Most excellent!

making art is one of the noblest, most difficult and highest achievements you can accomplish.

whether you are a

dancer,
musician,
writer,
designer,
visual artist,
or
director...

Artists change lives.

Without art life would be, well,

lifeless.

But before you begin your journey into the wonder of exploring who you are as an artist there are

3 rules

you need to know.

Rule #1

And this is the most important rule.

you
are more precious than your art.

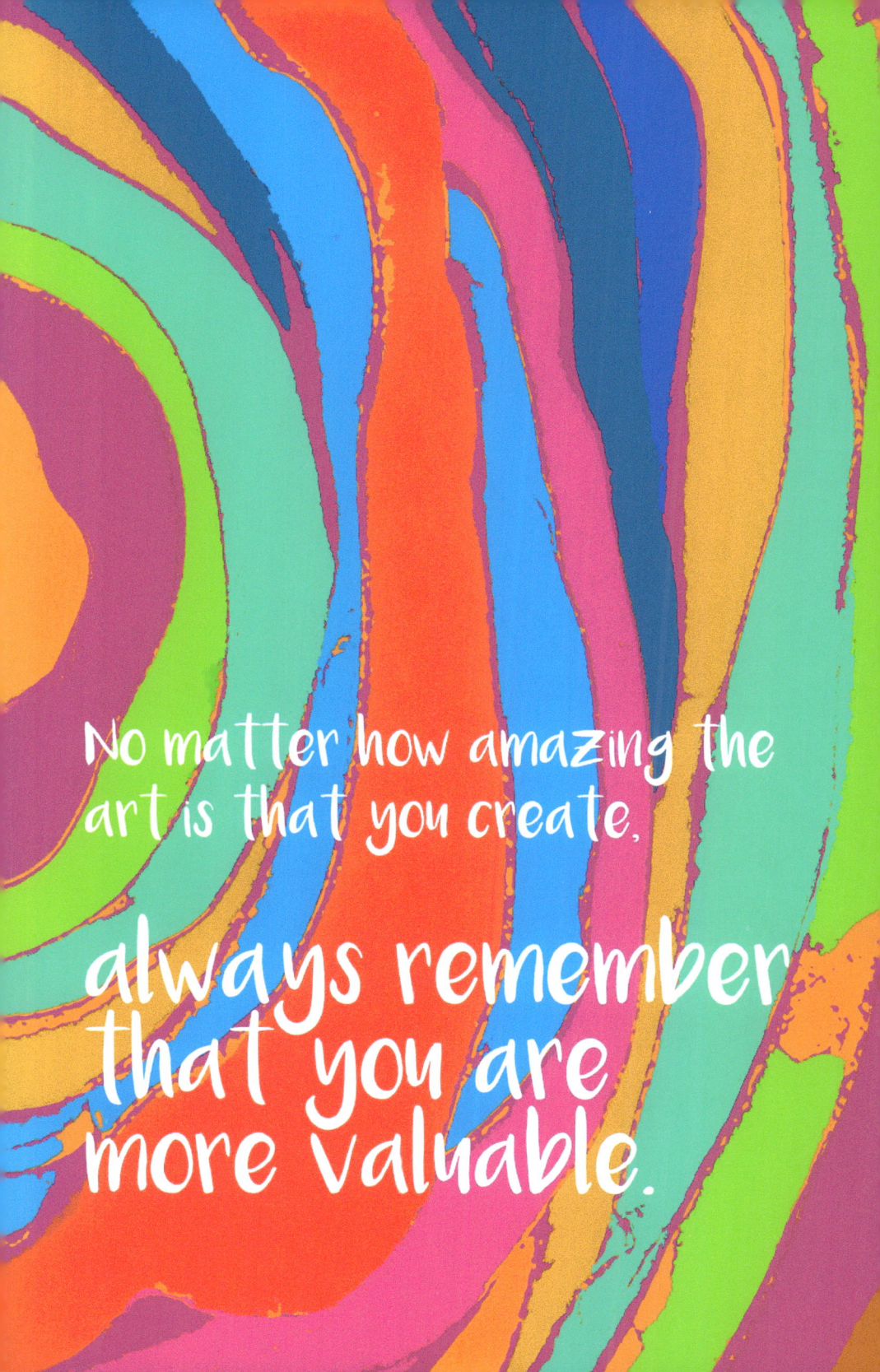

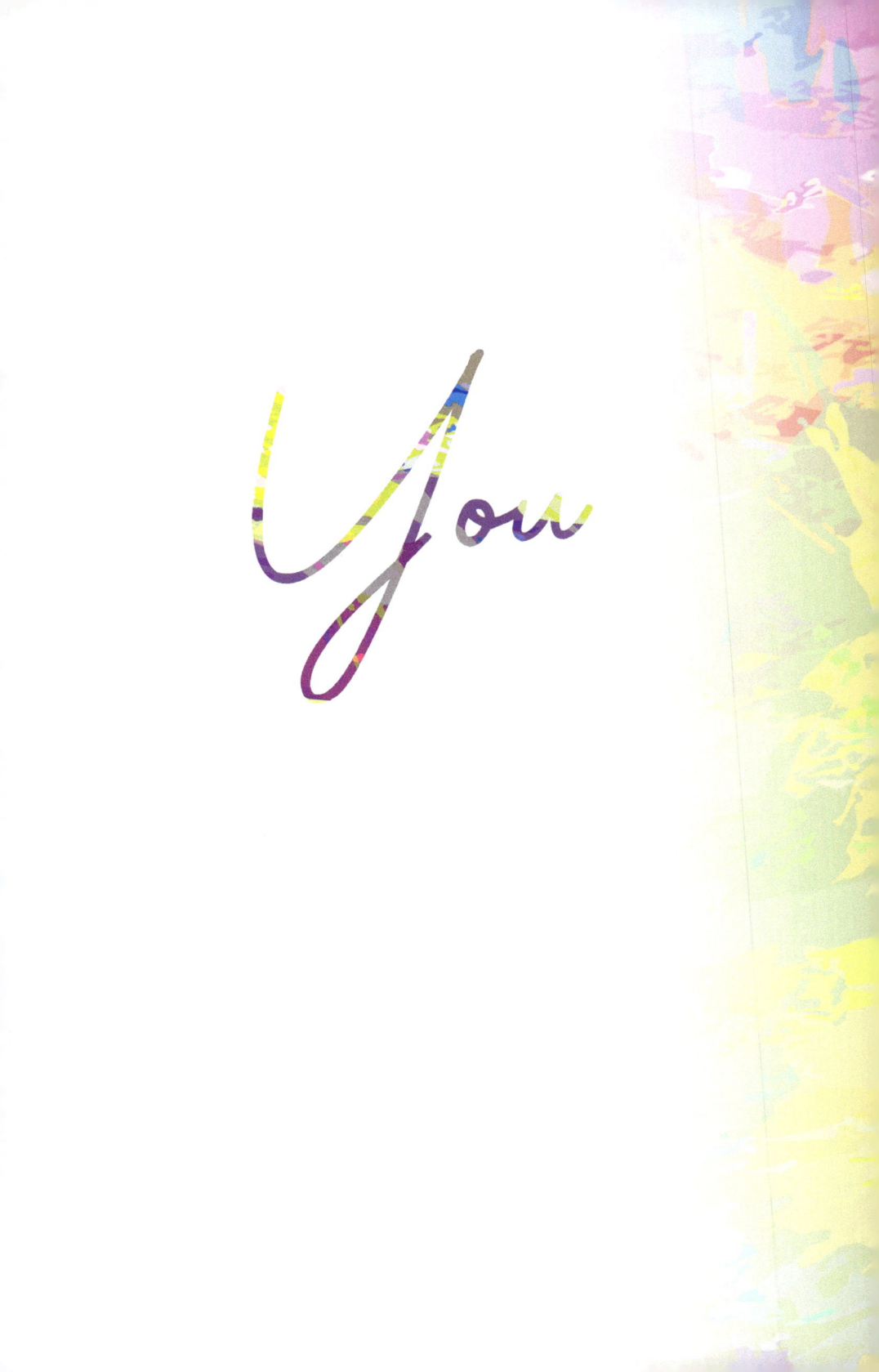

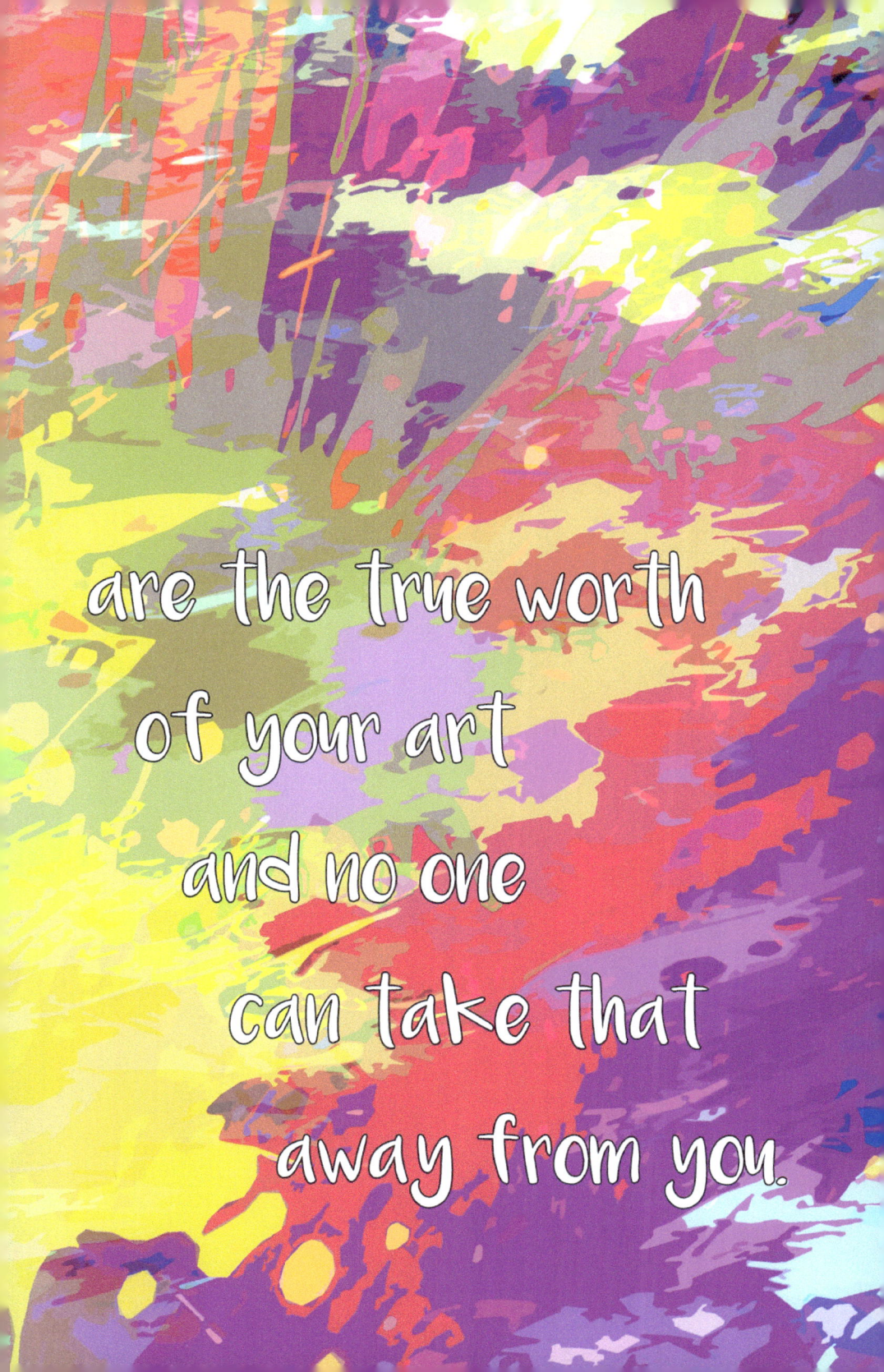

Rule #2

There are people who make a living off of convincing artists

that rule #1

is not true.

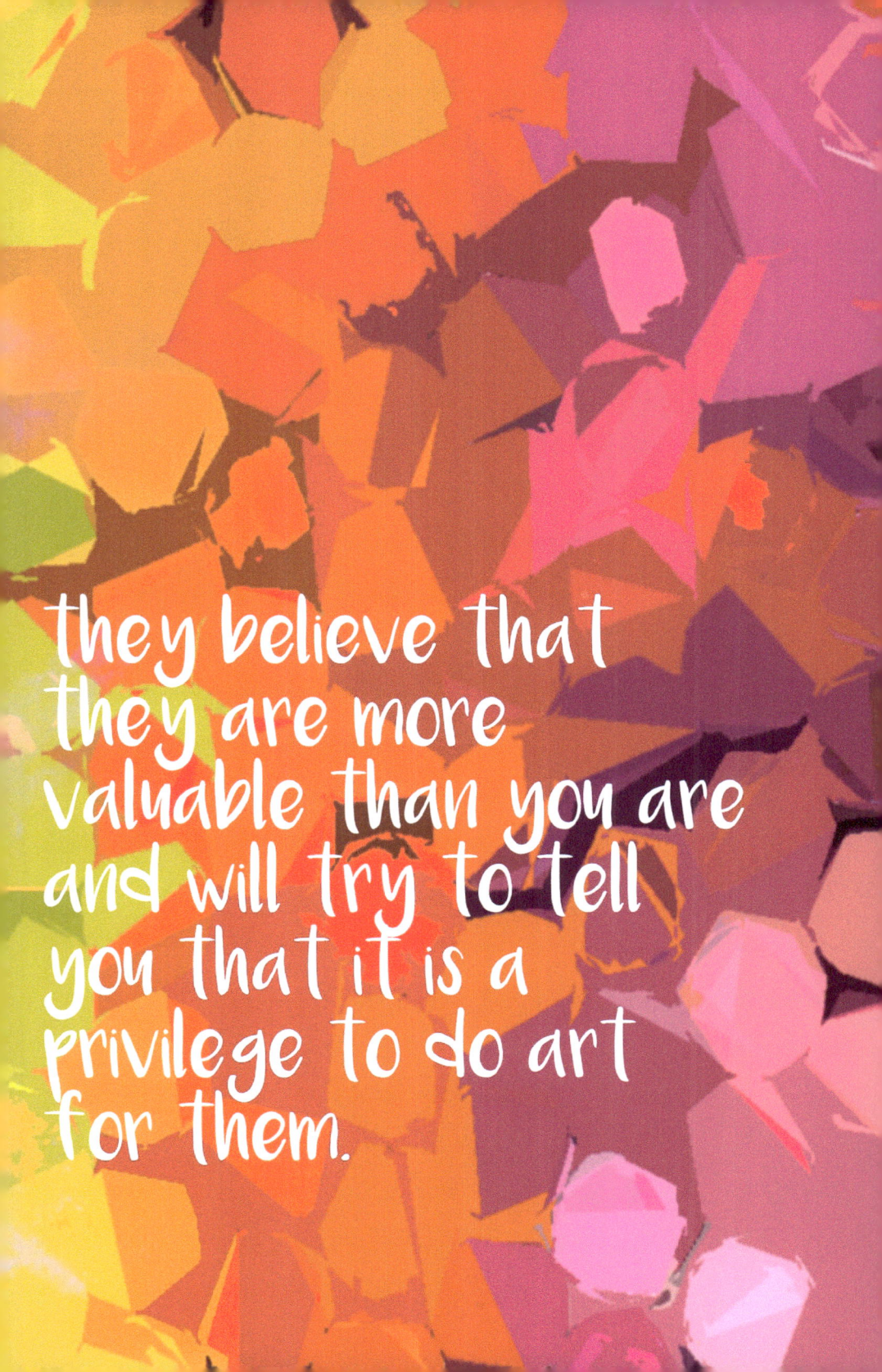
they believe that they are more valuable than you are and will try to tell you that it is a privilege to do art for them.

no matter what
anyone tells you,

try to remember rule #1.

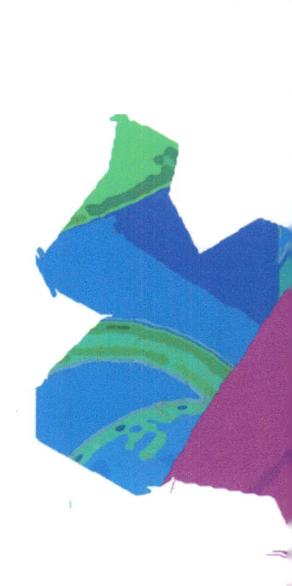

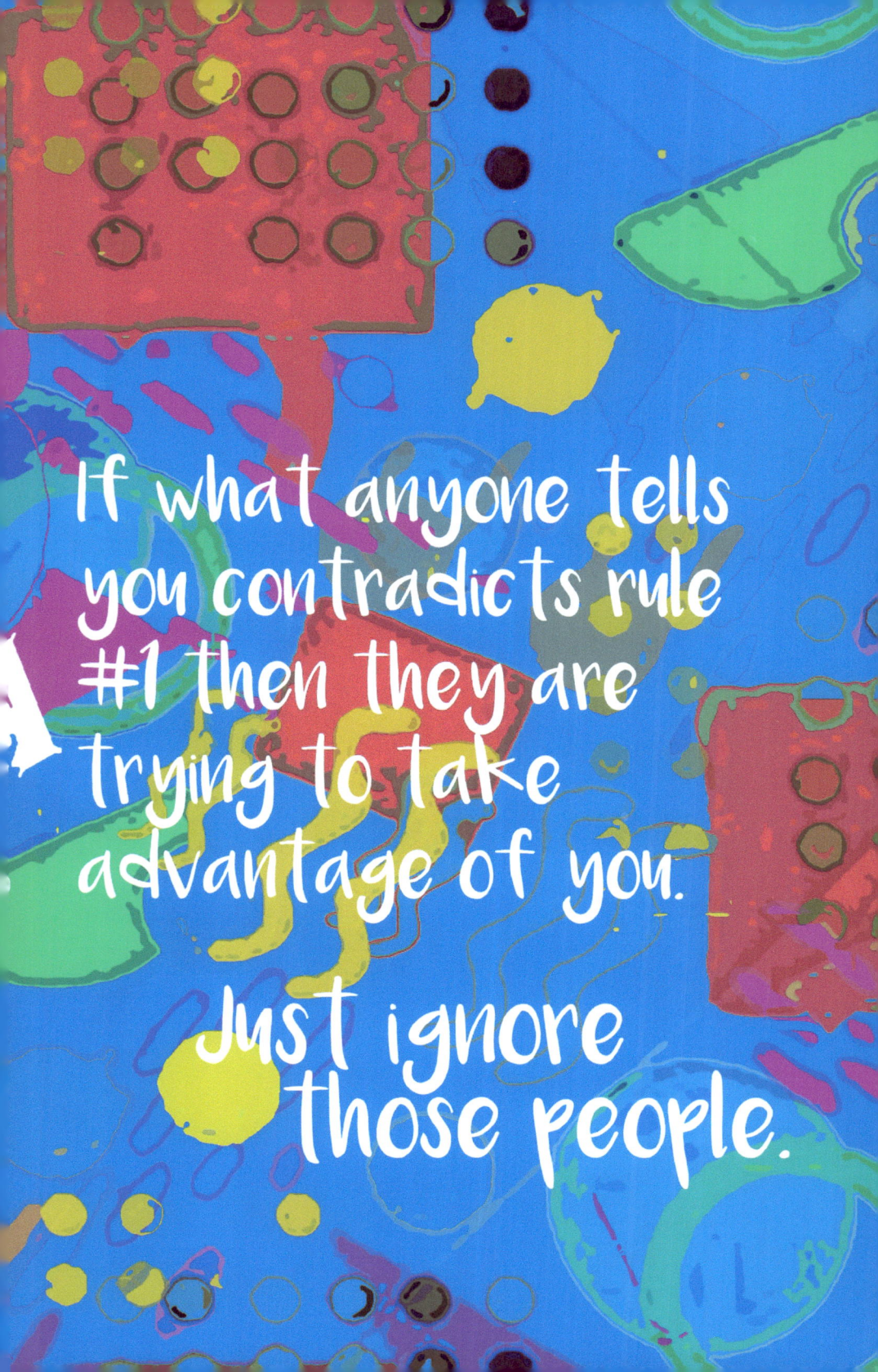

Rule #3

If you feel like being creative ...

then create

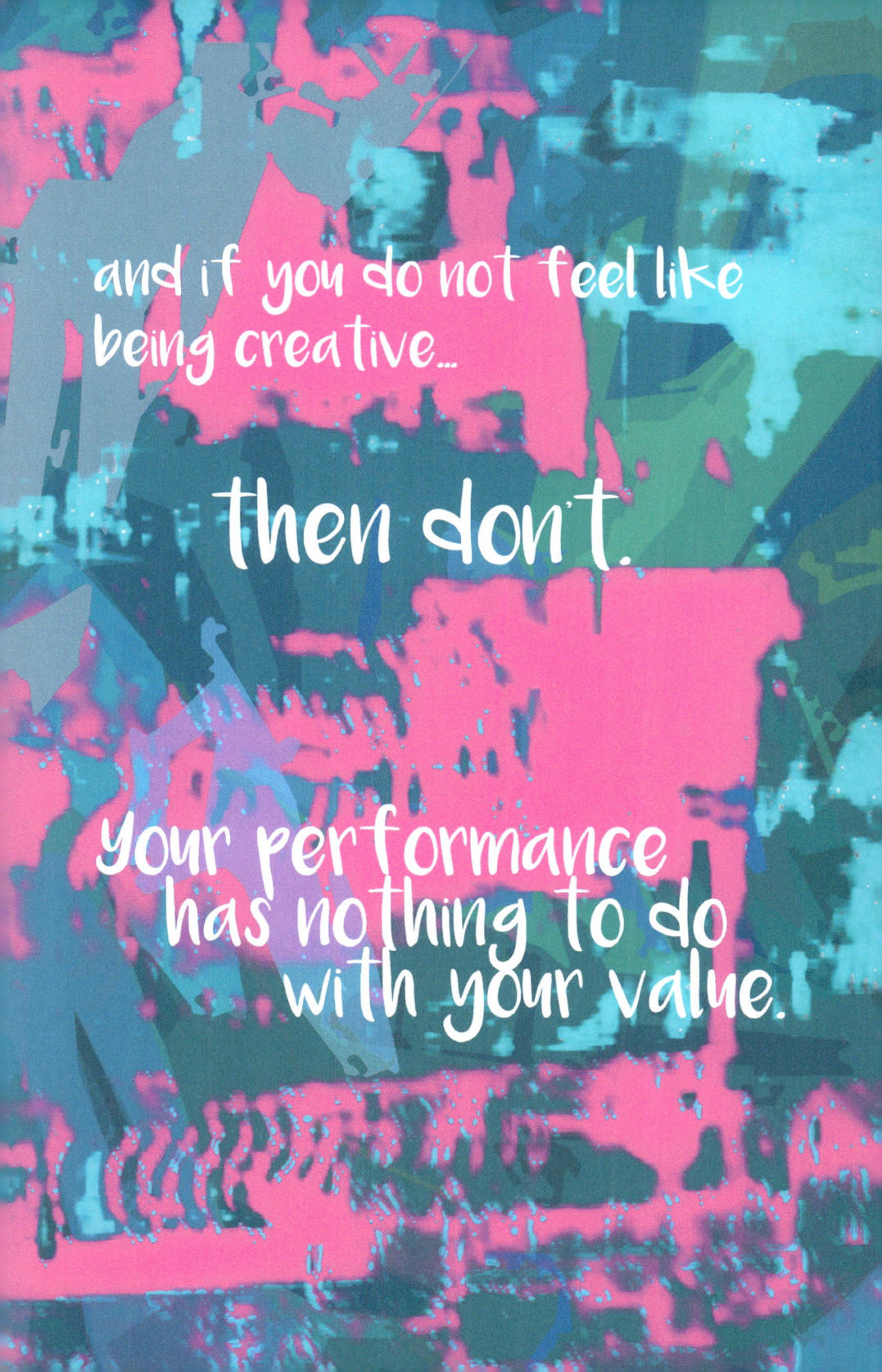

be creative
 with whatever is available
  to you

and let that be enough.

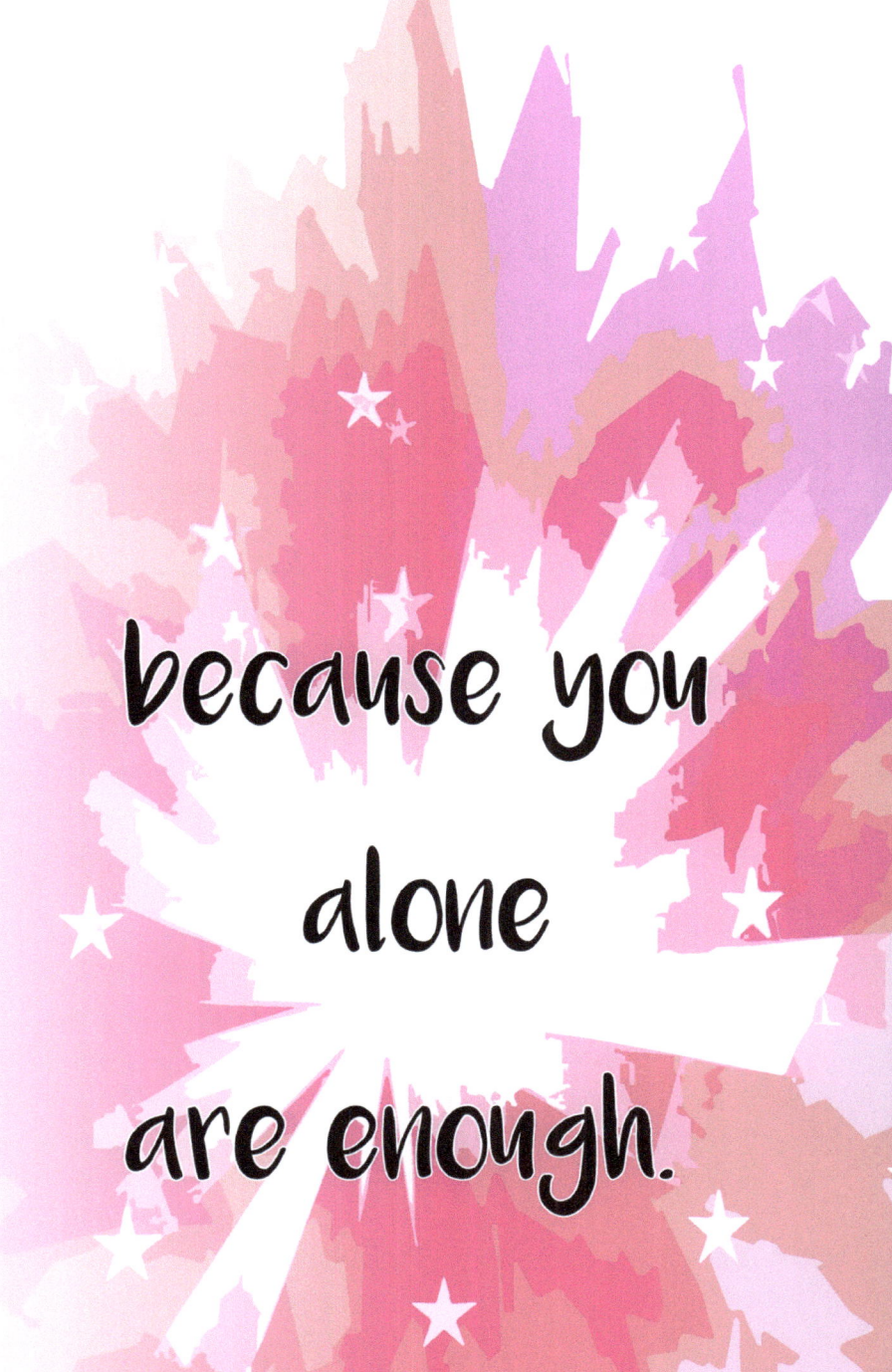

The next few pages can be whatever you want them to be.

Create.

Have fun.

Change lives.

Be you.

And always remember rule #1.

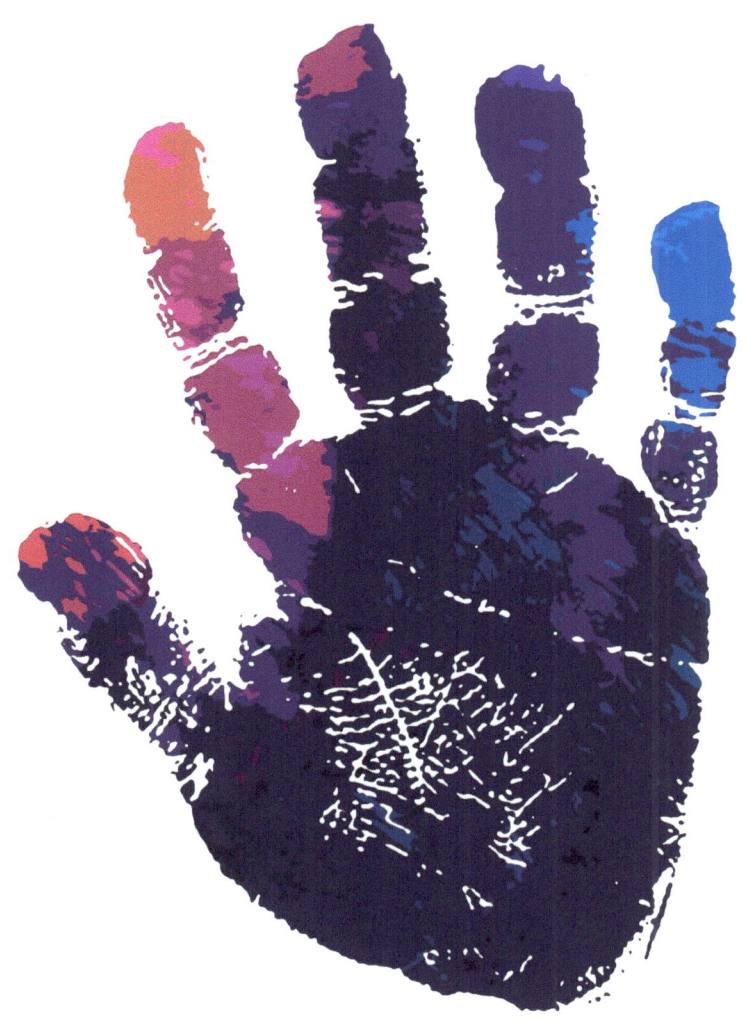

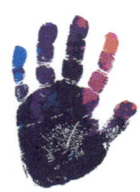

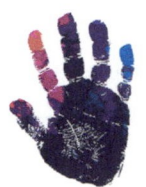

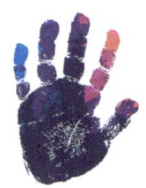

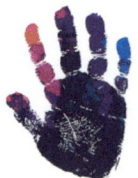

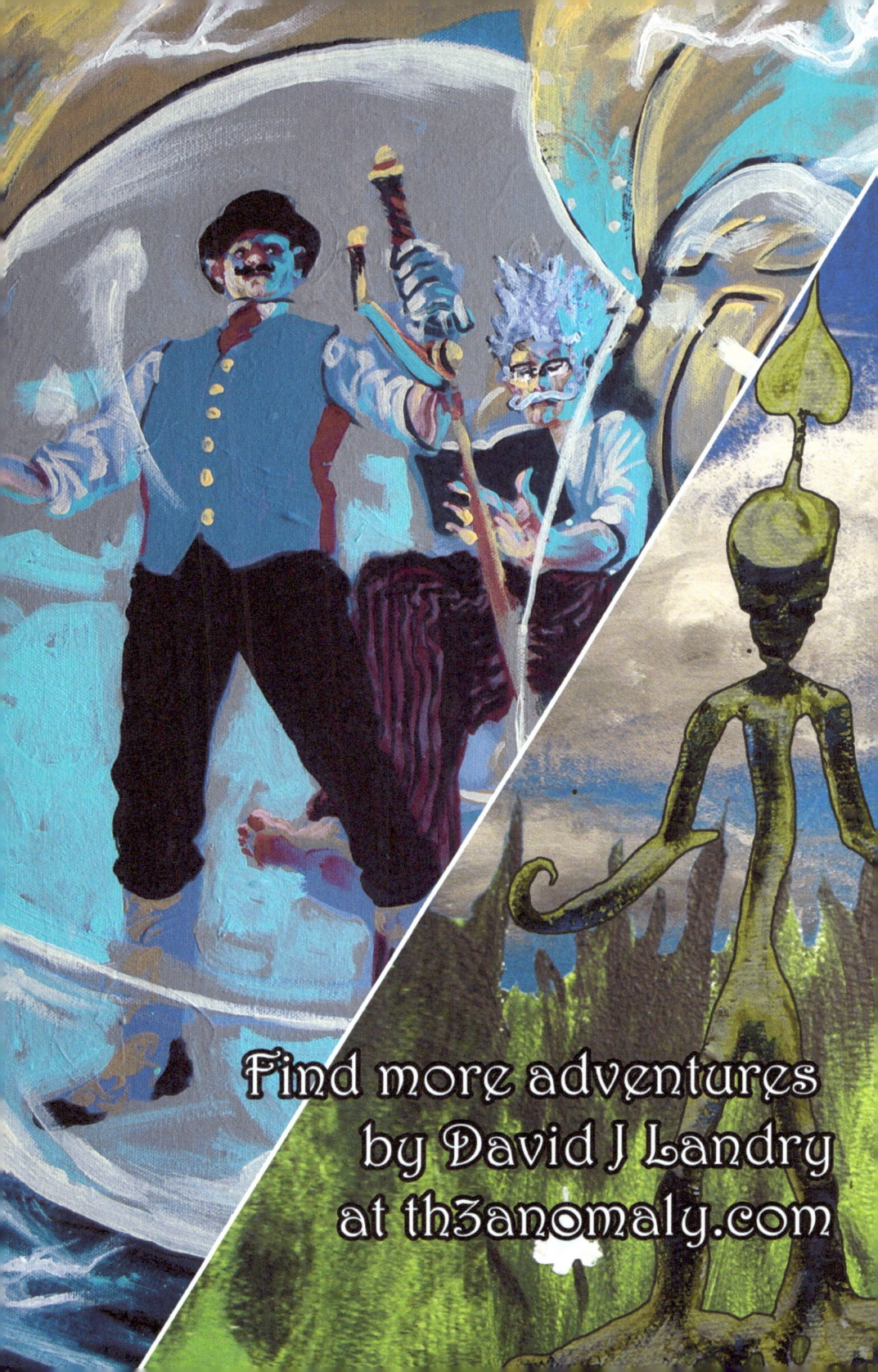